On the Third Planet from the Sun

New and Selected Poems

On the Third Planet from the Sun

New and Selected Poems

by

Stephen Anderson

© 2024 Stephen Anderson. All rights reserved.
This material may not be reproduced in any form, published,
reprinted, recorded, performed, broadcast,
rewritten, or redistributed without
the explicit permission of Stephen Anderson.
All such actions are strictly prohibited by law.

Cover design by Shay Culligan
Cover image by Colin Watts
Author photo by Patricia Ramdeen-Anderson

ISBN: 978-1-63980-634-8

Kelsay Books
502 South 1040 East, A-119
American Fork, Utah 84003
Kelsaybooks.com

Acknowledgments

Grateful acknowledgment goes to the following publications in which either the same or a different version of the following poems first appeared:

Amsterdam Quarterly: "Bloom"
Ariel Chart: "the makings of"
Art Night Books: "Rome, July 2012"
Blue Heron Review: "Threads of a Dream," "An Ode to the Moon"
Bramble: "Identified Flying Object"
Brawler: "Nighthawk"
The Dream Angel Plays the Cello: "Mission," "The Bearable Light of Invisibility," "Wordless," "Quest," "Ascent"
Fox Cry Review: "At the Oriental Theater in Milwaukee," "Legacy"
Harvests of New Millennium: "Blocked"
High Wire: "these dire, barely translatable, times," "Going to Visit a Dying Friend," "To a Leaf," "Some Things," "Nocturnal Charts," "Burnt Roses," "The Beast"
In the Garden of Angels and Demons: "On the Road to Mayo," "The Jingle Song on the F Train," "Baton," "Things Said," "The Place They Never Forgot"
Life and Legends: "Empty House"
Lothlorien Poetry Journal, Vol. 15: "Under the Olive Tree," "Bandwagon," "time is a curious messenger," "Fortitude of a Modern-Day Godiva"
Lothlorien Poetry Journal: "The Then and Now of It," "Betrayal," "Cosmos," "Telegram," "Voyages"
The Milwaukee Journal Sentinel: "The List"
Montezuma Resurrected and Other Poems: "Winter Wood"
Navigating in the Sun: "Swing with Chains," "Muted," "Reverie"
The Silent Tango of Dreams: "London Sighting," "The Privileged Secrets of the Arch," "A Gift of Lavender," "On a Hot Afternoon in Jerusalem"

Tipton Poetry Journal: "The Signal"
Verse Virtual: "Fisherman X"
Verse Wisconsin: "Reminiscence on a Sunday Afternoon," "Flight 006"
Your Daily Poem: "The Ancient Art of War in the Garden"

Preface

One realization that I have developed over the course of my adult life is that there is no geographic place that I can claim as my home. Rather, I have come to realize, much like the peripatetic writer, Pico Ayer, that I am really a person of the world, not of any one town, village, city or nation. My home is in my heart where my love and the love of others towards me reside, and that, on the scale of things, is what is really important and dear to me. Given my nomadic existence as a child living in different parts of the United States, my subsequent foreign language studies, Peace Corps experiences in Chile in the late 60s, marriage to a woman from the Caribbean, and my numerous travels and stint living abroad in London, I cannot help but have an international perspective and respect for other cultures.

I believe that the poems in this fourth poetry collection represent, to a large extent, this condition of mine, one that I proudly embrace like a global nationhood in this often confusing though fascinating world of ours. The world has offered me an international citizenship, one that these poems fondly embrace.

—Stephen Anderson

*Hope is the thing with feathers
That perches in the soul
And sings the tune
Without the words
And never stops at all.*

—Emily Dickinson

Contents

Bloom	15
Atacama	16
these dire, barely translatable, times	17
cornered	18
Pathways	19
Under the Olive Tree	20
A Poem for Frida Kahlo	21
Closing Up After a Bookstore Reading	22
Life Dance	23
Rome, July 2012	24
On a Hot Afternoon in Jerusalem	25
Muted	26
Residence	27
London Sighting	28
Quest	29
Nocturnal Charts	30
A Haiku for the Times	31
A Haiku for Night	32
Haiku for the Return of Spring	33
Reminiscence on a Sunday Afternoon	34
Voyages	35
Empty House	36
the makings of	37
The Bearable Light of Invisibility	38
The Match	39
The Signal	40
Going to Visit a Dying Friend	41
Five Six-Word-Story Poems	42
The Art of Not Knowing	43
A Gift of Lavender	44
Nighthawk	45
A Discovery	46
A Dance with Nature	47
The Beast	48

Reverie	49
Legacy	50
At Dusk	51
The Seer	52
Passing	53
Fortitude of a Modern-Day Godiva	54
The Hidden Chord	55
Fisherman X	56
On the Road to Mayo	57
The Privileged Secrets of the Arch	58
Blocked	59
Mission	60
Threads of a Dream	61
At the Oriental Theater in Milwaukee	62
City of Light	63
An Ode to the Moon	64
The Place They Never Forgot	65
An Ode to the Essence of Rubber-Bound Joy	66
Grit-born	67
Wordless	68
Up Kennesaw Mountain	69
Emergence	70
Derailed	71
Baton	72
centering a soul	73
looking for seashells	74
An Ode to My Daughter's Red Crayon	75
Unimpeded	76
Promises	77
Flight 006	78
In the Shadow of the Volcano	79
The Riddle of Them/Us	80
Gambit	81
Winter Wood	82

Telegram	83
But the Sky Is Orange	84
Sleight of Hand	85
Cosmos	86
Paradigm	87
The Ancient Art of War in the Garden	88
Sounds	89
To a Leaf	90
The Jingle Song on the F Train	91
Secrets	92
The List	93
Starburst	94
Identified Flying Object	95
A Pre-Fire Memory of Mass at Notre Dame (2018)	96
Bandwagon	97
The Then and Now of It	98
Burnt Roses	99
Betrayal	100
Showtime	101
Good Day	102
Some Things	103
undelivered	104
Time is a curious messenger	105
To a Wonderful World	106
Faith	109
On the Color Blue	110
Things Said	111
Ascent	112
Reconciliation	113
A Song for Earth from Outer Space	114

Bloom

An older woman walks her dog
down a bombed-out street in
Kharkiv. It's spring and she side-steps
cratered sidewalks with emerging purple
crocuses that magically seem to smile
their brightness. She stops, gathers her
breath, and listens to their quiet hallelujah
song, and bends to touch them as they
sing to her of hope and a smattering
of beauty—despite it all.

Atacama

I once hitchhiked north all the way from Santiago. Solo, unencumbered by the weight and distractions a fellow traveler would have brought. That set me free in a fantasy-laden time travel of many dimensions: truck-bed rider under the warm sting of hot, desert air, blue sunlit skies that tanned my skin; trekker over the crunchy desert sand and rocks; daytime and nighttime wanderer who found refuge at night in my sleeping bag nestled in between huge sandstone formations feet above the Pacific Ocean where I slept and dreamt about that strange land of copper dreams, never suspecting that the social and economic order of then would later change under thundered skies caused by planes strafing and bombing La Moneda during the coup d'état that would result in its President's death, followed by the hellish years of a dictator's atrocities, and the disappearance of thousands into shallow, sandy graves that would ghost them from the world, from relatives in need of closure. Had I been traveling the same paths subsequent to 1973, my experience would not have been so carefree. I would, in all conscience, have to tread that desert sand more carefully, so as not to step on any hand-bones emerging, sun-bleached and fleshless, their soft, muted cries for justice barely audible to me in my trespass of history there.

these dire, barely translatable, times

when to hold up an image
when to stand for that image
even when in your heart you know

its quaking in unreality
it is something thought to be known
but it is a conniving, pure, invention

something too convenient
something in excess of the rational
something nothing more than self-beneficial

fraudulent in substance
fraudulent in your very being
a fraudulent act that betrays you to the core

to the point that it perplexes you
to the point that you cannot in good conscience connect the dots
to the point that the time frame of your life becomes
untranslatable?

cornered

the path in the forest
seemed to lead to nowhere

rocks and sometimes boulders
along with errant rotted tree

branches challenged me
to tread their way towards

whatever notion I had in mind
that day, there in the godly

greenest of green rainforest
with its many distractions: the radiant

hummingbirds tapping
flower nectar without apology,

their wings beating to the pulse
of the lush flowered forest; the butterfly

color serenade to the land's beauty,
and I ask myself if these memories

will sustain me in years to come,
when I am nestled in some
megapolis reading under lampshade

about the modern, bent world we have
created in our ever madding pursuits

Pathways

Over that way on the way
to the other way, not this way

but that one that crackles
under those never-before-seen

lights that were lit that way,
not in the way we were born

into, but in the way of color
patterns thought to be unspeakable

in our way of perceiving because
our way never dreamed of such

alien visions, ones done the other
way, and so our way holds those other

ways taboo, in cahoots with darkness,
snakelike, tainted in their oh so

poisonous ways.

Under the Olive Tree

What is your legacy, Federico García Lorca?
Some say a stone marker under an olive tree
outside Granada. (Your remains have eluded
everyone, and your death is but a mystery.)
Was your assassin a vicious twenty-something
minion of Franco with unquenchable bloodlust
in his eye when he pulled the trigger that sent your
duende fleeing into blue heavens toward the Sun,
maybe into the hearts and minds of other poets
and playwrights attuned to fighting
fascism and injustice? Did your bell toll a knell
a las cinco de la tarde, like that of your iconic
bullfighter, Ignacio Sánchez Mejías?

Followers hope that your spirit did not die with your
body, that it flew like a bird and lodged deep within
humanity, much like a prolific rose of Sharon tree
sheds its seedlings to the earth to ensure its
propagation, like the sound of a gypsy violin
infiltrating the soul of the listener,
like the songs of Billie-who-sang-the-blues
that never, ever leave us.

A Poem for Frida Kahlo

There under the Mexican sun,
you, a mere child, felt the close
swipe of Death's steel hand after
fate led you onto that bus, the ride
that would exile you from happiness
and cast you into a bedridden angel
who would blossom,
like a butterfly from cocoon
there, corseted under sheets in your
cobalt-blue house,
into an artist mastering resilience
despite the shackled pain
of your shattered self.

As if early childhood polio and your tragic
bus accident, all later complicated by
your lover's roving eye, would destroy you!
You surprised the world by giving birth with art
beholden to no one—art with its self-
portraits, its reinvention of self out of the cripple
that the events had tried to mold you into.

You braved the Transmigration of Souls Highway
and flew on the wings of art as your escape
companion, and you invented angels in your image,
but that was no deterrent to your success
as an artist,
your real legacy in your turbulent world,
—in your Casa Azul,
your sanctuary in Coyoacán
that raised you from the ashes of your life,
and grew you into the splendid butterfly
that was to bless the world forever
with your very special kiss.

Closing Up After a Bookstore Reading

The lone bookseller's mind wanders as she prepares
the store for closing after the poet and audience have
left. But there is, in the emptiness there, an undefinable
presence, something sonic, magical, meaningful lingering
in that space and time—something alive whispering
secret things there in the dimly lit confines of the room.
And she felt sad with an awareness that everything
only has temporary residence when art is gifted
to any person receptive to it, and that everything
has only short tenure in the interpersonal realm
where all must end eventually, like dreams,
with lights out.

Life Dance

we are like the clouds
in that we transform, we shift
our presence, our very perceived
selves in our short shelved lives

in and out of our roaming, so much
so that we barely touch those around us
before the dance tune changes way
before we learn the song each of us

holds inside: muted whispers of fondness,
the oh-yes-I-see-moments craving expression,
somewhere out there on the plate of life
that is ever changing, in soft flow toward

a distant horizon where eye and word may
become one in ever so treasured moments
when two souls meet

Rome, July 2012

In the crowds, J. Caesar is invisible. He walks the streets of Rome as a shadow of himself, wades in the cool waters of the Trevi Fountain but does not make a ripple, reads the commemorative plaque outside the door to Keats' house at the foot of the Spanish Steps, listens to open-air chamber concerts in the Jewish Quarter near the Octavian Gate. He watches the feral cats *in flagrante delicto* where his blood was spilled by Brutus and his co-conspirators in the Roman Senate, now a lackluster, hard-to-find patch of weed, sand and crumbling stone. On Sunday afternoons, J. Caesar is drawn to the Colosseum, Vespasian's major opus; there, on the upper tier, he reviews the stone skeleton of what once was. At times like these, he wonders if fate could have been something different. Brutus, oh most contemptible Brutus! On Rome's many streets, Brutus' specter haunts him until one humid day when J. Caesar takes refuge in the Sistine Chapel where, among the works of Michelangelo, he thinks he sees Brutus in the horrified face of the man whom Jesus is casting to a devil in Hell. A smile erupts on Caesar's face, you know, the would-have-been *Rex* of the Roman Empire were it not for Brutus, all for the justice and deliverance found in one of Michelangelo's frescoes—Where else but in modern Rome on a hot, very hot summer day.

On a Hot Afternoon in Jerusalem

The sun-parched face of an old Arab
crowned with a kaffiyeh,
his nicotine-stained fingers clutching
a smoking Galloise,
peers directly at the
photographer.

Is this a survivor of untold losses,
of so many blood-curdling mourning wails
of Arab women,
this very same man who sips black coffee
sugared to taste from a demitasse,
a sweet companion to his cigarette,
a sure soothing balm for desperate souls
in such toxic, war-torn environments,
here during a sweltering afternoon in the calmer,
narrow lanes of a Jerusalem souk
where Arabic words dance between
walls, then flee, muted, into the open air?

Does he dream too—that Allah
will some day
silence
gunfire forever?

Muted

On the wall of my study hangs a gift
from a now deceased photographer
friend, a reminder, the picture, of the past
that currently looms like a specter of things
never changed, things once given quiet
lip-service over the years. The pain
in the man's face in the photograph
would be worse, undoubtedly, if he
were still alive—I imagine deeper
lines in his furrowed brow and jaw,
perhaps even a more intense glare
in his eyes at the contemporary world
he would be witnessing—after so much
tongue-wagging by all of those he wanted
to trust before to create hope for his
children, maybe grandchildren.

Residence

On the third planet from the Sun
stick-legged birds wade
in dried up marshlands,
water only trickles to quench
thirst barely, crops fail and wither
under scorching skies as snap-dry
harbingers of coming famines that
will test the human spirit,
all this shaped by a land of unbridled
greed that engages in its folly
of disbelief, a crassly defiant
and feigned ignorance despite it all,
a coma of disregard for the land's
dry-as-bone stream-beds,
beached and rotting sea creatures,
shoreline tarring due to flawed human
design in its myopic attempt to outwit Nature.

London Sighting

Distant descendants of prehistoric hunter-gatherers
now ride a train
sad-faced, beaten, civilized.
Separated from their ancestors
by thousands of years of progress
as evidenced by the smudged windows
through which they view their sooty metropolis,
humankind,
on a spiritual precipice,
dreams.

Quest

Under the starry net cast above
is the full-blown gladness of a Beethoven symphony
on a midsummer's night.
Here all is spoken in images at the juncture
of the lucid and the luminous where
transcendence pulls one into infinity,
where logic and pattern and ethereal
matters duel under impermanent stars
on slow-burn,
where the bioluminescent glow of fireflies
catch and hold the imagination along
with quiet majesty of cedar and poplar trees,
beach rose, mounds of moss—
where Nature is in her glory even through
the surreal fog of afternoon.
*We are all made of star-stuff. (Let us not deceive
ourselves: At least ten percent of all stars have
at least one habitable planet,)* dollops of rock
in perpetual time-slide,
and we strive to content ourselves
in the silky silence of our third planet from the Sun,
and amid Nature in her glory,
We inhale, we exhale.

Nocturnal Charts

From a distant hill
I've seen fireflies light
the flowering meadow
as dusk sets in.

I've seen motorists drive
without headlights on country
roads as if they were seeking
something in the landscape,
or in the night's clear sky.

After all, some things go better
without light, when the heart's
urgings rev up to decibels
of longing in dark hours.

I've seen evidence of souls
with their delicate wanderings,
there in the quiet of the night
awaiting its kiss of dew—their only
succor as beggars of the night.

There is magic in the air: the stars,
the fireflies, the cars, the errant souls
and the gentle kiss of dew now
enveloping everything, the lonely
roads leading to anywhere.

A Haiku for the Times

Teetering tense times
Ricochet through the media
Tilting at rich truths

A Haiku for Night

Sky glows burnt orange
Messages are sent flying
Sighs in the night sky

Haiku for the Return of Spring

The coyote struts
A turf claim is filed quickly
Crows take to the air

Reminiscence on a Sunday Afternoon

One sunny fall afternoon I, a man with no name, step out onto the deck to relax. It is an exceptionally quiet day, except for the birds that begin their birdsong without hesitation: I become their audience. After an unknown time there in my trance-like state, I realize that my coming out today was purpose-driven, that my left hand still clutches the garage door opener I had picked up on the way out. I give it a click. As the door opens grindingly, it does so with a screeching sound reminiscent of, as best as I can tell, Ennio Morricone's score for *The Good, the Bad and the Ugly;* I am suddenly under the rich blue Almerian sky in Spain where Sergio Leone cranked out that Spaghetti western circa 1966. Silence . . . no bird song. Just a man with no name now transported to the mesquite plains of Almería, dressed in cowboy garb atop my stallion next to another pale-faced rider—Clint Eastwood—who, with piercing blue eyes and a small cigar between his lips, glances over at this man with no name and says, "Sorry mister, I got to get going . . . You coming with?" For unknown reasons, I stay put as Clint rides off down the dusty road, his six-shooter's blue metal glistening under the Spanish sun. Black out . . . return to my backyard birdsong, I with no name am seated exactly where I was before, garage opener in hand. The uncertain fate of my garage door is seriously pondered. I pause a moment, but then I click the opener impulsively, so I can hear Morricone at least one more time.

Voyages

I watch from my hotel balcony
as a sailboat in the distance

sails its course under a radiant,
powder-blue sky on the great Tagus River

whose shoreline laps the enchanting
city of Lisbon.

Its sails are billowed with enough wind
to cut through the sea-like river inlet

from which Vasco Da Gama voyaged
in caravels fitted and funded

by the Portuguese Crown ages
before this tranquil scene below—

the magical seven hills of this city

of *Calçada portuguesa* and colored
walls now kissed passionately

by *Fado* sounds throughout its narrow,
cobblestoned streets singing its

paradoxical blend of despair
and hope.

In the distance, the sailboat seems to trace
the sea explorer's path off into the blazing sun.

Empty House

The other night
I dreamt I visited Isla Negra
but Neruda was not there. Only
formations of strange seabirds
skittered the sky above, rocks
whispered secret things of protest,
and the sea waves spoke in tongues
that burned clear through my heart there
outside the poet's maritime palace ransacked
by Pinochet's marionettes ages ago in search of
truths they could never understand. I dreamt
that the tree I sat under dropped leaves
with poems written in blood-red ink. I
caressed the lush earth there, and read its sheaf
of leaves accompanied only by the song
of the sea's rising tide issuing from Neptune's
throat.

The night's air at dusk
consoled me with its sweet, hypnotic voice
and cool embrace under the slate-grey sky
enshrouding Neruda's dark island, and left me staring
in awe as I attempted, in desperation,
to stuff the leaf poems into my coat pocket,
but they crumbled and fell to the ground,
reuniting with the earth that so generously
gave birth to them in the cycle
of that poet's vision.

the makings of

let there be no mistake, we are
bejeweled by the stars, by their
stardust and radiance, atom by atom

being sold short is of our own making,
not theirs, as we all climb the tree of life,
branch by branch, its illusory permanence

inspires us all, even with its shakiness,
its faux green aura that we seek
to repair because inside we, like it or not,

are the anointed ones who are star-baptized
and capable of truth-gathering about this
shimmering, breakout world

The Bearable Light of Invisibility

The man in the shower couldn't help but notice several hard points as he lathered his underarm area, first on his right side, then his left side. Overcome with curiosity, he instinctively scratched the layered skin around them with his fingernails. His efforts to rid himself of them continued, shower after shower, but all proved futile. His thoughts about the curious bodily changes were at first amusing, to say the least, but eventually the reality of his plight caused him to think in ways he never suspected he was capable of. A veritable parade of bizarre thoughts cascaded down upon him. Thoughts like was he growing wings of his own, certainly unlike Icarus who had to make his own out of bamboo and silk, or he was being transformed into a facsimile of *Birdman* like that portrayed by Michael Keaton in the movie of that same name? Maybe too, he wondered if the forces at hand in life itself were casting him to become a creature like one of the angels conjured up by Rainer Maria Rilke, the Bohemian-Austrian poet, whose poetry inspired Wim Wenders' movie, Wings of Desire. The man pondered the above, and concluded that, if he had to choose, that if he did eventually change into some winged creature, that he become one of those all-knowing, beneficent angels like those in the Rilke-inspired Wenders movie, an angel of mercy, invisible but able to comfort those in distress. The man concluded such a new chapter in his life, that of a silent hero capable of rescuing the otherwise tortured souls comprising humanity, would be well worth his conversion discomfort. Thereafter, instead of scratching at the hollow horny shafts as they began to emerge from his sides with increasing semblance to feathers, he stroked them gently as if they were becoming his wings of hope. After all, he concluded, immortality is bound to have a price.

The Match

You who burn into the black night
lighting the darkness with your

being amidst the racket of the world,
your solitary flame fighting the fickle

nature of those who share their space,
time and energy jousting at their windmills

of uncertainty in the disconnect between
their take on life and yours, a match where

hardheads collect, and try as they might
to snuff out your flame, all the while cheering

on for an envisioned wasteland, the one
shepherded by their evangelic idols who

capitalize on their every ill-conceived
promised land.

The Signal

A five hour road trip and three hours of moving my daughter back into her dormitory have left me hot and tired, a refugee in a downtown Minneapolis hotel. Nevertheless, I feel obliged to call an elderly aunt whom I have seen a total of four times over the last quarter century. When she answers, her reedy voice quavers with a peculiar tone of strident urgency, and she asks . . . no, she insists that we drive out to visit her and my uncle at their west-side suburb, really the last thing on my mind this humid, smoldering late-summer afternoon with threatening-looking rain-clouds already thundering across the plains off to the west. So I regrettably decline her frantic request and tell her that such a trip would be nigh on impossible, which is something that my aunt does not want to hear because she obsessively repeats her wish with her former urgency now turned to a tone of sheer desperation. A captive of exhaustion, I do not take the hint, nor can I hear her real message, the one vibrating up from her heart like a call from the other world to which only she knows she will soon go.

Going to Visit a Dying Friend

The road there seems long
With the roadblocks of thought
That creep and lie in wait
Like potholes and detour signs
Wanting to mess with me
As I try at every turn to focus
On the purpose of this trip
A pilgrimage to rescue and comfort
A soul longing to cling to hope.
I swallow hard trying to forget my own
Long-standing separation issues
That are cruelly fingering me with a sense
Of ineptitude, but which challenge me
To rise up in martyrdom to the cause
But Deep down I know I will glide
Into the expected role, the one cast
By a director of the unknown now
Taking a foolish chance on me.

Five Six-Word-Story Poems

(1) Beyond

Gray tenement walls. Blight. Graffiti enlivened.

(2) Yard Saga

Squirrels. Nut holes. Pockmarked green lawns.

(3) Summer Deliverance

Boredom. Butterflies flitting on flowers. Enrapture.

(4) Threesome

Writhing worm on hook. Fish. Done!

(5) The Hat

Not worn. Closeted. Dust collection protest.

The Art of Not Knowing

things they come in a sequence:
a collapse of a romance,
a shattered heart lending itself
to a terrain of loneliness,
a tearing island within you,
the catatonic recluse with a dream to be alive,
radiant under the sun, with gratuitous
sightings of magnificent whales
and, all the while, an excruciating sense
of lack, with things gripped in a longing
like that captured by Hopper in which things
stay open with a thirst for the unforeseen
instances of life, not entirely knowing
that not knowing drives science
and is the essence of art in this world,
a mere speck in a constellation
of mysteries.

A Gift of Lavender

A beautifully potted lavender plant, a
gift from a poet-friend,
has begun to wilt and turn color,
despite our good attention and untutored
nurturing, like the mysterious
disconnect that sometimes occurs
between a leukemia patient
and his nurse. It has begun to march
to a strange, unseen drummer, much to
our great sadness and sense of
loss, prompting us to prepare ourselves
for a unique, very special
bereavement. We have planned a decent
burial for it in our backyard next to our hearty
rose of Sharon tree. We hope that
the tree's roots will savor the
lavender plant's delicate, recycled
company, a wedding, we think, that
will breed an irresistible lavender
Hibiscus brandy, a sure-fire elixir
for the honeybees next mid-summer.

Nighthawk

It's 3 AM outside the 7-Eleven.
In the distance, approaching car headlights
Dot the blackness at this hour while
Inside a scrawny twenty-something sits
Behind the counter tracing a 9 mm under
The counter with his fingers, surrounded by four lonely
Walls that contain items insomniacs seek
During black hours like these. All the cars
Pass silently except for one that booms by, its radio blasting—
A rolling boom box that shatters the still,
Vapid night air while the car's occupants
Head to nowhere good, to their rendezvous
With the nothingness of this night rhythm
In the key of absurd loneliness.
They all seem to head toward what home
Might be, the place where eyes will later
Strain under desk lamp far into the night
Amid silver ghosts that shimmer in the dark blue
Shadows before sleep envelops them in a dream
Of star-sent angels light years from Edward Hopper's
Nighthawks, while outside the night's mist slowly
Evaporates as it will again and again . . .

A Discovery

Last spring the old bay window over the back deck was
Done in by ripsaw, crowbar and sledgehammer—
Smashed into a pile of scattered debris on the deck.
Among the leftovers, in the middle of the boxed-in section,
a hornets' nest rose up, a Taj Mahal dome in miniature, some ten
Inches in diameter, a delicate looking carp scale pattern of maple
Seed and other unknown matter, home, the carpenter said,
To scores of yellow jackets many of which terrorized us in
Seasons past while we entertained on the deck.

When the nest was torn open, its interior was empty like
Some lost, ancient civilization once sheltered so well by its
Intricate design. Now gone forever from our property, a sacrifice
To our sliding deck door, a weatherproof invention—
Man-made technology of high order, lacking though, the
Miracle that preceded it in that spot.

A Dance with Nature

In the snow drifts of winter woods,
our footsteps' sure sounds against
snow-packed twigs sing for us a crisp
song, accompanied by the wind through
the evergreens and the leafless tree tops,

all lending evidence of a feast for our senses
in this time of our otherwise jagged and jarring
realities far from these precious sojourns
with Nature in all her gifts to be found

under the canopy of the bright blue sky above,
now radiant beyond our wildest imagination in this
very special communion, one capable of giving us
an uplifting rebirth—if we only give it license.

The Beast

Ever so often
It can be spotted—
The solitary,
Scraggly coyote cutting
Through neighborhoods
Wherever it is called by some
Mysterious force of nature. It
Invariably gets no respect:
Unsympathetic drivers honk their horns,
Neighborhood dogs bark their warnings
And kids think maybe that it'd be cool
If the beast intruder could only be
Hit by a passing car, so they could get
A closer look, maybe kick it or something.

Seeing all of this makes me side in secret
With the perceived pariah, as I follow him in his
Determined saunter down our street while he looks
For God knows what, like a bestial Quixote
On a secret mission to restore some natural
Order in this, our world together.

Reverie

The stars—the very same ones
that I imagine beheld by my wide-eyed
German and Norwegian ancestors in the early
1800s—now shine on me, brightly
as they did then in the Midwestern north
country where those relatives built sod-houses
on their tracts of land with their calloused hands,
sweat-soaked and with grunting determination, not
too far from where I, some time and distance later,
sit watching Shakespeare under that same canopy
of stars, a smile of wonder on my face while caught up
in the intrigue of the Bard's play, the cicada serenade,
the late summer cool caress of night air—
a communion with something
not totally known there.

Legacy

No easy task this
Cleanup of basement workbench
Full of multifarious clutter,
Dusty mementos of hand-me-downs.

The real chore is in tossing the
Handmade tools my father
Crafted as a machinist under
The final shadows of WW II
And the scraped-up pale-blue tackle box
Full of Lazy Ikes, Bombers, Jitterbugs,
River Runt Spooks, and
Hula Poppers.

A simple matter on the surface
But what's not seen is
The slippery thought of
Letting go of steel craft and memories,

Lovingly bequeathed as if
They were brothers whose being
I'm now releasing like unwanted
Fish, letting them drop from my hands

To the trash bin below, letting them go
While I suppress a traitor's smile,

Great Judas at the workbench, son
Who is not much more than an ingrate
Who will probably keep only the tackle box
In the end.

At Dusk

In the fields around us
The pitch of crickets plays out
In the key of D, a quiet whistle,
Sweet by the friction of their wings
That means rain as the clouds
Above dim the moon and we
Are spared lightening and thunder
So that a lesson learned here
Is that we are not everything
Or grand in this natural refuge
In its gift of a wet embrace. Our
Story is but one along with
The other creatures here as
We seek, through a faint light
In the distance, a clue of what
We are going towards.

The Seer

Go away, nevermore to come
while candles flicker in the breeze,
beholding the largess of some
as some are born into disease,
sinister faces are brought to bear
before the magnificent ones who insinuate
amid shadows in deep, dark air
under that umbrellas do berate.
But there is a caller in the beyond
whose eyes are wide open
who calls all the aspirants around
to summon forth their faith unbroken,
which will allow those ones driven
to set free all hearts from their prison.

Passing

Not of this world but the others,
our origins come atomic and gritty,
a stardust-drawn and blown
to an Earth-land crawl aspiring
to some point of being, of shimmering
elements amidst the nothingness
in imaginary tokens of conjoined
creation,

or so we assume in a continuous bout
with uncertainties, and we adapt and gather
incremental knowledge to guide us into
the Great Dance as things pass from one
to another to another . . .

And all the while, we spy on and scan
the stars ghosting away above in the heavens,
and with reverence, we secretly
mourn the passing of their magnificence
when we allow ourselves to see them
with the curiosity of the heart.

Fortitude of a Modern-Day Godiva

The female in the picture—a middle-aged woman—
Has her hands firmly gripping the steering wheel
Of the wide-bodied, vintage vehicle she got
From an elderly man eager to sell it for, one might
Say, a pittance, but that's so typical of her crafted cunning
That from the get-go as a child has had to navigate
Difficult life-maps: loss of trust from age six on; a whole
Parade of rocky, loveless relationships in sprees
Of two, three, maybe even four, all desperate attempts
To shake, rattle and reform the angst of her existence
That had hardened her to a heightened vigilance
And her secret stewardship of other disadvantaged
Beings that have somehow wandered into her
Life, in desperate need of her generous, very generous
Mentoring and life-marshaling.

The Hidden Chord

have you ever noticed
how a woman gifts to the world
her woman's dance
in the quiet hours
of our loneliness? when she
opens herself that way,
are love-struck dreams at
the helm? when the dust
of the day settles in this broken world,
is her battle with life
lifted on the wings of love landed?
so much has been delivered, so
much forgotten so, in that process,
I ask you, is it not held afloat when
the woman in our life extends
her hand, and whispers *family?*

Fisherman X

On one end of the pier in Talcahuano,
a fishing village not far from Concepcion, Chile,
fishermen gather around the side of the pier
and a commotion ensues for something being hauled
up onto the pier by another man in a boat. A body,
large and rigid, like a huge fish, is shoved and pulled
headfirst above the lip of the concrete pier. The man's head, its
eyes open, seem to stare into the dawn's brightness,
a cruel reality between his night and day,
after he had set out the night before in his trawler
in search of lobster, abalone and sea bass to sell
to the fish mongers for the morning market.

He who caught from the sea was himself claimed,
a trophy catch by the elements of his life to which his body
surrendered unwillingly—perhaps due to a slip, a heart attack, a
trip on his boat enough to send him reeling into the pull of the
cold, black sea.

And now, laid out with his sea-worthy clothing
and rubber boots expelling their slugs of sea water
on the dock, there perhaps mocked by his enemies,
grieved by his friends, in his respite from all standing
above him during his unpredicted ocean-side wake.

One wonders, at moments like these, if there are silent cries
of lost-being and dreams issuing from the corpse's open mouth, if
they recount sweet and harsh memories, if they might be food
for a memoir that will never be.

On the Road to Mayo

The road itself across Wisconsin, then the western banks of the Mississippi River consoled us—we took backroads—a scenic, snail-paced journey devoid of numbing interstate rushing and bug-spattered windshield. Mick Jagger rocked us with *Satisfaction* while we both took in the sights on the winding drive along the river, going north on the Iowa and Minnesota sides, stopping briefly to watch a bald eagle glide into a majestic dive to snatch a large fish from the water. The riverside bluffs on both sides loomed like stoic, timeless guardians of the river treasure flowing below. We stopped to admire prairie flowers a little farther up the winding road, crossed the flat, black-earthed Minnesota farm fields and drove on through the rolling prairie land until we finally entered the Rochester city limits. Famished, we found a roadside cafe where we prided ourselves in ordering and devouring greasy cheeseburgers and sipped malted shakes, just like we did when we were love-struck grad students many moons ago. I couldn't resist the old juke box there so I slipped two quarters in the slot. As Jagger sang *You Can't Always Get What You Want,* in the distance we could see Mayo puncturing the late afternoon sky, a place full of busy magicians in that Mecca of hope, now shimmering in that ever so reachable distance before us.

The Privileged Secrets of the Arch

Of all of those in the park, only
The rosy-cheeked, disheveled woman saw
The Poltergeists weave under and around
The monumental park arch, so much
So that she dropped her plastic bag
Filled with everything she owned
And cherished, thereby setting her
Hands free to applaud them as they
Set about in their anarchistic abandon
Magically whirling debris with whistling sounds,
Creating traces of colored lines that were
Utterly magnificent for this lone observer
To behold. What a shame—she thought—
That she must relish in this free performance
Art alone. And how blessed she considered herself
That only she could enjoy such a gift in her very
Own dusty, litter-strewn amusement park while
Others there could content themselves with just
Simply staring at her.

Blocked

Just beyond the sandy crest
Dates bake in the sun,
Water is poured into tin drums,
Children watch their fathers
Stroll away down roadsides.

And those children, bursting
Inside with angels and demons,
Wonder about slingshot throws,
Feel impervious to real bullets,
The threat of demolition by
Bulldozer, soldiers who think
Of them as animals—each side
Out of touch with their Semitic
Muscle fiber, their similar genetic
Codes, despite the different paths
They have taken to the same place.

Each other's sweat is not seen.
Each other's blood is not seen.
Each other's life is not seen.
Each other's family is not seen.

There is only blindness, at times
Blistered by the sun, at times
Chilled by cool and rainy winters
With rivulets of water inhaled
By the waiting parched earth.

Mission

There was a man
of erudition and moderate distinction,
of modest south side Polish
Chicago origin
who became a Jesuit,
then an errant suitor
with a drive for status
through women, an eye
for a climb from his
childhood backyard.
Twice he married
only to be rebuffed
by Fate in which guardian
angel was the inscription
of his name: caretaker of sick
and fallen souls
who chose his attentive
company.

Threads of a Dream

Chicago's little sister-gem of the Rust Belt,
just up the Lake Michigan shore,
south side church spire-sitter of historic
parochial neighborhoods, one proud basilica, a world class
four-sided clock tower, cradler of a once great
Menomenee tribal culture, home to beer and iron baron
dreams, factories and German, Polish and Italian
immigrants of the 1800s who forged New World hopes
over Old World fates, city of transformation
and melting pot experiment,
a city not yet fully defined, merging with the African American,
the Hmong, and the Hispanic imprints of this century—
Milwaukee is wishing, hoping, a historical incubator
of mind-expanding activism and vision—
igniting now towards take-off
to a new century.

At the Oriental Theater in Milwaukee

Something tells me that the little man
in striped short sleeves and a Sears' tie
could really cut loose with a wild, wailing
boogie-woogie on that awesome Kimball concert organ
on stage down at the Oriental Theater,
instead of the *take-me-out-to-the-ballgame* / true-blue schmaltz
he is probably told to play before the previews come on. Not that
there's anything patently wrong with his standard repertoire, but
that magnificent organ has got to be capable of so much more,
as I'm sure the man is.

Watching him play, I can imagine him suddenly exploding
into a Ray Charles or, hell, even a Jerry Lee Lewis rocking
rendition in which he shakes the sleepy, popcorn-eating, soda
swilling place up a bit, maybe even bringing those exotic moldings
and fixtures to life
before the main feature sparkles from the screen.

And so, every time I'm sitting there waiting for the big screen fare,
I'll imagine how nice it would be if he could, just once,
snap out of the corral he's in, out of all that has been constrained
inside,
and make hulk-like
all that stuff
barely breathing there.

City of Light

Above a poetry venue in its dungeon house,
Paris lives
in its mysterious cloud that borders
between a dark, bloody history
now aspiring
            to angels,
and a *joy d'vivre* coupled with culinary delights,
from Victor Hugo's visions and Monet's famed "lilies,"
this incomparable city
looms proud,
defiantly resisting ennui of any kind,
an intellectual hub of life-changing
science from Pasteur and Madame Curie,
architectural consistency,
it is poetry incarnate,
cobblestoned and iron-grilled,
culturally evolving into its
own dome of perfection that is
eye-popping by the volume of its
sheer ubiquity.

An Ode to the Moon

The moon is still
a snow color
as it shines its majesty
with a sober air,
there distant but
omnipresent in its arc,
whether in quarter sliver,
half-moon,
an imposing three quarter
form or full-faced and bold,
it radiates a magical spin
on our insignificance,
and our moody dance
with life—insinuates
its presence over
our fondest dreams,
our never ending folly.

Peace be to thee,
oh moon of always,
there nestled
in your shelter
of night black.

The Place They Never Forgot

The rotating barber's pole lured those seeking a haircut into Hank's place, but so did his legendary fame as the best barber in his neighborhood. Veteran customers knew better than to expect what you might typically regard as a barber full of friendly repartee or child-friendly comments—Hank was gruff, a grumbler at best, and seemed to live in the world of opera solos from Verdi's *La Traviata, Aida,* and Bizet's *Carmen* that serenaded him and his customers, sometimes in scratchy renditions of their godliness that echoed from an old phonograph atop a nearby table. It might be a reasonable assumption that Hank generated many future opera lovers (or haters) as a result, and that most, if not everyone, loved or, at least, respected him. He did it Hank's way—bare bones, no frills, and he gave you what you really entered his shop for. When you left Hank's domain, with your neck powdered and your hair freshly-clipped, groomed and with that famous "a little dab'll do ya" stuff, one could not help but feel like a recruit given reprieve to exit again into the glare of the afternoon sun, ready for the onslaught of crazed girls who couldn't wait "to get their hands into your excitingly clean, disturbingly healthy hair now so full of life"—until shagginess would again give you your marching orders back to Hank's place.

An Ode to the Essence of Rubber-Bound Joy

Distanced from the child
we once were,
we sprint along through life
with our dwindling fascination
somehow bereft of that primal joy
that the young child
in us once possessed
to unimaginable delight
with things as they are,
unfiltered visions of things
in the environment: Think
a helium-filled red balloon
floating around the room
becoming a mouse to their
cat, a bone to their hungry dog,
something meant to be savored,
savored fully in the truth of
the thing, altogether objective
takes on the images before them. But
the meanderings of time and events,
so incalculably complex that they draw us
out of the immediate, the enjoyable
moment at hand, robbing us
of that valuable part in this life,
this world in space and time,
and a child's much needed center
of gravity within the gyroscope of life.

Grit-born

(for girl X in a war-torn zone)

Do not mistake
What I know as
Innocence-bound—
Never for a minute
As my young eyes
Have seen it all.
I survive,
I sing like a songbird
From the cage of war
I survive,
And my soul flies free
To the heaven
Of my dreams.

Wordless

I remember the red brick house
Of my childhood in Atlanta, &
The pale, almost ghostlike image

Of my mother, perpetually in bed,
With frail arms with just enough strength
To gently hug me, caress my hair
When I, her freckled-face cherub,
Ambled into her domain there & broke
Her silent self-vigil.

I remember taking leave of my marble games,
Creek-swimming, tower-climbing, & my forest treks—
My entire 7 year old existence—when I sensed that she
Might be calling me, like a sweet siren, so that she could again
Stroke my hair as I nestled next to her on her bed,
As I, with a sense of something I didn't understand,
Submitted instinctively to her timely,
Ever so timely beckoning there.

Up Kennesaw Mountain

A ragtag batch of boys made their way
up the north side of the Kennesaw ridge,
in search of mini-balls, pistol parts
and any other conceivable remnants left
weathering over the past century in Georgia
red clay, once the war instruments
that belonged to the clashing Union
and Confederate forces whose blood—
the boys concluded—made the clay there redder.
And the boys' imaginations sparked
with notions of that battlefield where
thousands lost their lives as now a place
ghosted by the fallen.

For the boys, it was a magical place peppered
with the lure of newfound war souvenirs—
a holy grail for those boys—soon to become
desktop trophies at home,
symbols of the mad sacrifice of war.

Emergence

There goes the car carrying
mom and dad with 11 year old
son in the middle seat
of their 1952 shiny, black Hudson
four door sedan heading out toward Nashville
with mom driving and dad a passenger,
and it's a bright, sunny day trip
for a family to see relatives over
in the city they were destined to head
for; the ride is remarkably smooth
in their extra heavy Hudson, and mom
handles the steering well, so much so
the boy doses off leaning against his
father's shoulder.

Rounding a hilly curve, mom does not see it right
away, too late to swerve to avoid the massive truck
looming toward them in their lane, attempting
to pass another car in what had been the truck's
lane. Dad, in a microsecond, throws his body
over his son, and after the deafening crash, the boy
awakens to his bloodied parents, and with all his might
pushes his lifeless father back into his seat, and cries
his mother's name, but she too is lifeless.

Life, it seems, is like that: a collage of the beauty
of those tender moments, the utterly unforeseen outcome
of that day when the boy's father was called upon
to commit the ultimate act of bravery to save his son.
We walk through whatever doors are opened for us by others,
and greet whatever persona that may be waiting
patiently in the afternoon sunlight there,
shining, shining on, for us.

Derailed

A toy train diesel, a Lionel 1615 circa 1955,
Has been resurrected from its coffin box,
The one it shared its departed status with a few
Of its tracks and a transformer in the basement
Until this afternoon when I sought it out on a whim—
I'm not really sure why.

So here it is in front of me, well preserved,
Still with its gray-black steel skin and its undiminished
Mechanical allure that captured my boyhood fancy,
Now a mere specimen on a table,
A 61 year old piece of sleekly crafted metal toy,
Attempting to rekindle my childhood fantasies
Of a happy, intact family gathered to witness my mastery
Of its noble distraction from events yet to come
That would have the power to bury it in its box
Never to be looked at again
Until now . . .

Baton

On a grassy rise adjacent to a footbridge, small children speckle the spring grass during a short respite from their classroom, some rolling full speed with arms flailing every which way—some with cautious, almost deliberate half and full turns while, above on the knoll, some women, mere shadows against the sky behind, watch over them. They look from child to child as each child navigates the slope. Chances are they are not as want to pay too much attention to the willy-nilly rollers who, with their oxygen rush, will not get injured, much like drunken drivers who usually sustain only minor injuries if any. Instead, it's the slow rollers, the overly careful ones that are red-flagged by the attending adults because they are the ones who are injured the most, their little uptight twists and turns predisposing them to broken bones, ankle sprains, a clobbering or two from collisions with the willy-nilly ones who flatten them on contact because of their wild abandon. Just how much the flagged ones will learn without their caretakers 'advice becomes part of the myriad choices parents must face as they sculpt and mold their loved ones into the adults that will someday tower over *them* in life, and watch *them* in return, lovingly, thoughtfully in their circular dance.

centering a soul

there was a time when the bobber and sinker
were set just so.

when hands older and more skilled
than mine

could maneuver the earthworm—
twist and attach it to the hook,

when the line was lowered
below the water,

when in the mystery
of that silence together,

something more than fishing
was quietly imparted, shared

when the Zen
of that moment

blessed us
with its gift.

looking for seashells

the sand hides part of their
depth, the color and patterns
of their sea-made exoskeletons
of calcium carbonate shelter
created by a delicate array
of creatures vulnerable to the ecosystems
that support them.

their discovery on beaches is
a joy for us, especially for the curious
children who pluck them
from their sandy beachheads as
joyful discoveries which become
bedroom collections for those
whose imaginations fuel dreams

of the sea, fantasies of Jacque Cousteau-
like affiliation deciphering the ocean's
boundless mysteries aboard the Calypso,
sailing into the dangerous escape offered
by breakers that slam seawater onshore
so that seashells, spike-over-crown, are tossed
into the sandy beaches there, jetsam from its depths
that showcase its truth with its glistening frame
of beach sand.

An Ode to My Daughter's Red Crayon

It's crazy what
your silly red wax
can do
when in the hands
of a terrible-twos-kid.
Such messages
you deliver
on virgin white walls
wherever.
A censor
must be
called in
to modify
your humor.
They're all there
now though—those
radical, obscure x's,
circles and Picasso-like scrawling.
And yet
my daughter defends
you, you dirty
red crayon, you.

Unimpeded

The three year old boy in the park
stops repeatedly, oblivious to his parents' impatience
in their wish to move on to their cherished, more important things.
The boy's vision is not limited like that
of his parents' selective attention that blinds them—
to the plump yellow-black caterpillar crawling
on a ficus leaf, the red-crested cardinal
gracing a park tree with its sweet song,
the sleek jet-black Harley parked at the curb,
the formation of ants crossing in the crevice in the sidewalk,
the tickling touch of of a tree branch against his arm,
and the sweet smell of the Daffodil bulbs—all of which are
keeping the boy from this hurried world, and its
madding call.

Promises

Outside puffs of wind twist
and curl the blue kite, tease

its twirling ascent, its only thrust
the string-pull by the six year old girl

while her grandfather palms
it between forefinger and thumb,

patting it afloat against the resistance
of the wind, but an oncoming

car cuts short the girl's energized,
full-of-hope run down the street.

But there is always the chance of a replay
of that summertime duet, a ballet really

between two frolickers caught up
in their mesh of irreplaceable kinship,

under the sun, on a semi-windy day.

Flight 006

I did not really believe the thin *porteño* seated next to me on the flight from Santiago to Buenos Aires when he leaned into me with an elbow-tap and voluntarily confessed to me that, in all his years as an air traffic controller, only once did he experience a UFO, one that five months before had hovered above the glass tower of the main airport in Buenos Aires for what seemed like a frozen minute before shooting a laser-like beam that cleanly pierced the glass tower just seconds before it flew off and became instantly invisible. I noticed the peculiar way the man with the pencil-line mustache nodded as he narrated his tale, as though he were trying to convince himself of what he had just related. After all, grabbing a stranger on a plane to tell all that to was, I thought, marginally bizarre if not downright so. And to add to the strangeness, we later parted with just a handshake as we exited the plane once in the land of the *porteños*.

This life is undeniably full of enigmas, not to mention quirky people, so *flake* is the word-impression I had as I glanced across the carousel as he appeared to be in a deep state of impenetrable thought, oblivious to everyone and everything around him. I retrieved my bag and exited through Customs never to see the man again.

As plagued as I was at the time by what might be described as the Peace Corps Volunteer wanderlust syndrome, I arrived about two weeks later back in Buenos Aires after my travels up to Uruguay and Brazil with just about enough money to pay for a flight over to Mendoza, just over the Andes from Chile where I needed to return like three days before. It just so turned out that there happened to be a U.S. Air Force base there where two U-2 pilots adopted this feckless wayfarer for three days before paying for a taxi-van up over the Andes to Santiago. As they were driving me to that taxi, I related the story about the man on the plane, and, as I was doing so, they looked at each other and grinned.

In the Shadow of the Volcano

(Peru, 2023)

The blood came
From where sweet wildflowers grow

Who would have thought
Such births on mountain sides

In the idyllic passage of spring,
With its sun shining on hurt

Hearts with grievances roiling
Deep inside from the mud-role

Of their yearnings gone
Unfulfilled century upon century?

Such is the fall from inner grace
Rocketed by time and hidden

Patience worn thin by quiet pleas,
By petitions of the heart pumping

Something other than status quo
Forever.

The Riddle of Them/Us

I am me to you
I am I to me
What you think
May be
But
You don't really know
My true tribe, i.e., mixed,
Homogeneous, et cetera—
Nor I yours.
Shaky perceptions
Create mirage-like images.

We don't really know
The other
Person's
Dreams.

Over river, lake, land and sea,
We battle our inclination
To not fall

Into sheer folly.

Gambit

those people of the coco
& mango
once flew, oral tradition tells,
on the wings of giant macaws
from where they reigned terror on those
who encroached on their
sweet liquid honey lives, those who
wanted to scrape-rape their
land & people under the sign of crucifixes
on mission walls,
something not easily portrayed
in the acrylic & pastel renderings
of artists today, settling to just capture
the dusty recollections of it all.

Winter Wood

Branches & twigs
become glassy ice thorns
erect against the wind,
ally with the tempest, & become
another musical component
of the wild harmony
of the woods in the thin blue air
of a winter afternoon.
God's breath
an icy wind is.
It just is.
No questions asked . . .
no questions asked.

Telegram

Sometimes the river is calm with a glassy smile,
but when it imbibes too much thunder rain,
it becomes nasty-tongued and curses
its riverbed with sloshy slung mud
and river flood, cracks levees
with the force of its flow and its reckless
mindset, one that some struggle
to explain away with physics, but I suspect
that somewhere beyond that science-faced
rationale there is still one tough God-of-Havoc
trying again and again to tell us something
supremely vital and raw.

But the Sky Is Orange

Each day
when the Sun's
wink at dusk
signals
yet another day's
passing,
we quietly praise
its colors
over what horizon
life offers us
under its spell.

We cannot disregard
its reality, its
adversities when
purity of air
is side-railed
by smokestack clouds
and grit expelled
by industrial dreams
fed by sham innocence
riding the waves of today
and tomorrow without
the slightest regard
for the one part C
and two part O haze
engulfing this third planet
from the Sun.

Sleight of Hand

So many mysteries
are spun

Inside a mere drop
of water

Seemingly so pure
and taken

To refresh our flesh
body of self.

Invisible are the
alien elements

There hidden so well
in the water's

Crystalline essence
we think above all

Reproach until microscopic
analysis spits out

Some ugly reminders that
all is not well there.

Cosmos

I admire wildflowers
They bloom bold,
Often with brazen
Displays of color.
I especially cherish
The fact that they
Burst forth in full bloom,
Unaffected by the war.
Pandemics besiege
Humanity as if we,
On the grand scale
Of things, don't matter
That much anyway. And,
Come to think, the follies
Of humankind have ravaged
Our planet, and the flowers
Have not.

Paradigm

Hot summer days bring out delirium,
or is it reality perceived in the garden
of life?

Strange how the child in us can be so captivated
by the wonders of hummingbirds hovering
like miniature helicopters seeking succulent

flower offerings during the afternoon
swelter. Undeniable is the soft, sweet
offering of flower petals—even

proud rose stem thorns that act
as soldierly sentinels, the guardian angels
of such delicate beauty there, forever-stamps
on roving spirits seeking something
in the radiant glow of afternoon sun

where uncertainty is somehow
magically checkmated in the transient

moments spent there—a solace
granted—no questions asked, none at all.

The Ancient Art of War in the Garden

The Greek mint has begun its ruckus again in the backyard.
I have tried to teach it to lower its voice, but it has paid no heed.

A Japanese maple, rose of Sharon tree and a flash of flowering
    bushes,
while maintaining social distance, have been cringing but tolerant.

The cedar board deck, aged and grayed by its years, yet handsome
and commanding, serves as a mute border to the proliferating
    garden growth

that is really, admittedly the hub of color-swirl and herbal takeover
there. A copper wind sculpture, faded green and with its double
    helix

patterns formed by the gratis compliment of wind on a spectrum
from low—high, can only co-exist, a metal figurine to be toyed

with by the weather, subservient but oh so enduring and
    statuesque.
And, all the while, the aggressive Greek mint's roots wrestle
    with its

adjoining floral brothers and sisters, and won't allow
for a three-count during its battle for soil nutrients, fierce

and ruthless, like Achilles conquering Hector there in my
suburban garden, a veritable Troy to that race of one

undeniably aromatic, Greek herb, its only *heel* being
vulnerable to the trowel shelved and waiting in the garage.

Word in my house is that its fate will be not death,
but solitary confinement in a yard pot in a remote, distaff

section of the rock ecosphere there.

Sounds

The gliding sound of the walker wheels
on the waxed, tile flooring,
interrupted only by the muted
clack sound
of the walker's placement
by the woman walking there,
slowly down an isolated hall, all
with an erect posture,
patiently navigating there
with an irrefutable
grace, a solo performance making
her a master of exercise ritual,
one day at a time, an image
on this day beheld
only by this stranger who is captivated
by her elegance and determination
to not let go within the cocoon
of these protected, hallowed walls.

To a Leaf

I, like you, am changed by age,
curled at the edge, bent forth,
humbled by the force of wind.
I shift around from one place to another,
seek out new harmonies with Nature
in all her seeming fickleness through
the seasons. We both are mysteriously
drawn to her tune, ready to do our
similar yet unique jigs
every time.

The Jingle Song on the F Train

An old woman (homeless?drug addict?destitute?)
on the subway train stood to sing
her a Capella rendition of "Lean on Me"
with a plastic cup in hand.
Like most rogue buskers, she was perceived

as yet another petty annoyance on the sweltering
train late at night, but her singing
began little by little to infiltrate
the passengers' awareness and drew some,
—as the spirit grabbed them—
to clap in rhythm and sing along
to words like ". . . We all need somebody to lean on . . ."

While no Ma Rainey,
some donated spare change to her but I,
deep in a conversation, had none
so the best I could do was to smile and nod
my appreciation (or was it sympathy?) as she
glanced my way when she walked by.

And the woman sang on, before
exiting with a toothless smile, her cup far from full
as she shuffled on to the next car.

Could it be that something might be all right
for her   somewhere at the end of the line?

Secrets

Invent me a story
The dying man said—one
I haven't heard before. Explore
The sound of a tin drum
Or the arc of a bald eagle's swoop
Into water for fish prey, or
The meaning of the earth-born cry
Of a birthing mother just before
Partum, or
Explain where the colorful,
Delicate birds go when Midwestern
Winter cracks the air with frigid bite.
Tell me where all the world's religions
Intersect for I suspect that is where
The core of all beliefs may be found
If one exists, and why the monoliths
Of Stonehenge were configured so.
And, young man, do not leave out whey
You and I are the same, yet so different.

The List

Now dear, do not forget to pick up the following: one-half lb. of aged Manchego (so much rides on this ingredient!), six celery stalks, 25 oz of chicken stock, a small bottle of extra virgin olive oil (just virgin will simply not do!), one Vidalia onion, at least two garlic cloves, 30 oz of chickpeas (you'd be a DREAM if you could only find the Trinidadian one!), one chili pepper, one bunch of curly kale (not the regular kale!), and one half lb. of chorizo sausage. Sweetheart, I could have used these things about two hours ago, but do your best, okay?

So after 53 minutes of store time in no less than a total of five stores, I arrive home with the above ingredients, panting as I lug the bags in, and she sighs in one of those Oh-my-God-I-can't-believe-that-I-forgot-to-tell-you to pick up 2 bottles of Rioja Reserva! No sooner than she has uttered the last word of that regrettable statement than I am walking to the corner liquor store, a neighborhood adventure, well, at least a walk with what most probably will hold some cardiovascular benefit for this man of errands. I have always admired the idiosyncratic architecture of our area.

Starburst

After some further thought,
I think that Lorca had it right
during his sojourn strolling
around New York City
in the summer of 1929, tongue-tied
in amazement at the shuffle
of pedestrians, the skyscraper landscape there
with its thousand girder-high buildings gnashing
at the glimpses of sky above, building ledges
as refuges for hawks desiring a rest
from the cavernous streets and honking
cars, its noises and smells bootlegged
from everywhere, mind and poetry
boggled by the bold furnace-
breath of capitalism at its most
rampant gallop, one that clouded
and lent itself to Lorca's poetic
jumble with which he tried,
at his then debased best, to make
sense of it all. Today the city's
mask has changed in many diverse
ways, but the throbbing pulse
of its raw-energy-boom staggers on toward
shifting images of its own making.

Identified Flying Object

Dear neighbor-to-the-north of mine ~ It is with
Utmost high regard that I would like to inform you
Of the presence of your son's whirligig flying object
That abruptly ensconced itself into the interior
Of my pride-of-pride, Grandiflora rose bush,
And in the process
Decapitated a couple of the most radiant, rosebud clusters
That had previously adorned my otherwise barren, lackluster
Backyard. Well, I just wanted to say, *no worries!*
And that I well know that accidents do happen,
Especially when kids somehow magically channel their
Monsters and demons in healthy, outdoorsy ways.

Please retrieve said son's IFO, preferably ASAP.

A Pre-Fire Memory of Mass at Notre Dame (2018)

Paris is rainy grey. Refuge is found inside Notre Dame which is cool but drier than its exterior guarded by a bevy of 19th century add-on gargoyles that are said to ward off assaults by harmful spirits to its Gothic exterior. Impressive, I think, and fantasy inducing, but here inside I feel absolutely nothing nestled next to hundreds of Parisians and tourists, devoutly enraptured and praying all around me. Nothing at all, even with the accompanying choral music, the priestly maneuverings up in front on the altar. Despite the cathedral's immensity and Gothic appointment . . . nothing. No tears because of its material beauty or the community of humanity there before me. Only tolerance for what I imagine passing through the minds of the religiously inspired and believing among me, which is not to say that I don't admire the devotion that they exude, but I just simply cannot make it. I am more inspired looking at Monet's collection of *The Water Lilies* just a stone's throw away from this looming church. And then, of course, there's Victor Hugo's House, The Picasso Museum not to forget the history of Paris replete with lightness and some very dark events during the French revolution. Blood from the Church passed to the streets where it coated many a pavement with blessed tragedies of turmoil that ultimately resulted in the Paris of today, preserved but now in its spectacular lightness from that darkness. And the Notre Dame mystique now spirited here between these walls that box in all these trappings of Gothic splendor, all for the Catholics who remain somehow, mysteriously to me, enticed. The hellish fire of 2019 most probably did not squelch their religiosity in the least.

Bandwagon

When my great, great grandmother set out
From Baden Baden, Germany on her way
To the New World, one looking back at that can
Only struggle to fathom her motivation and intent.
Why would anyone want to leave such
An idyllic place with its green promenades along
The picturesque Oosbach River? Its thermal springs?
The beautiful scenery bordering it for miles around?

Questions arise: jilted maiden embittered and humiliated
By her patriarchal society? A catchy ad in a local newspaper
Promising great rewards for immigrants willing to risk
Everything in the expanding American frontier? Did she leave
Traces of herself in ironed, neatly-folded clothing
As reminders of her missing status so that she wouldn't
Be forgotten? was she fleeing family complications as
An unmarried young woman two months pregnant?

Genealogical diagrams give only snapshots, but the true stories
Of our ancestors surface only as tapestries—
Moth-eaten by time, most likely loaded with mysteries
That could nourish our curiosity forever.

The Then and Now of It

I went to clean my father's tombstone the other day.
Kneeling there a meadowlark's sounds came my way
and gave company to a gentle breeze that tousled my hair,
along with a sunlight that enlivened me there.

But my eyes teared while transfixed upon the blackened stone,
and with scrub brush and water and soap I washed it so
that its granite face sparkled aglow.

Slowly words were uttered there, words like *I miss you so,*
words lost in the muted silence there on the cemetery hill,
so that a fusion did occur in the air in a slight chill.
I apologized in a prayer-like voice the sadness of my guilt,
and I made a pact, in the silence there, that true
diligence in the future I would prove.

Burnt Roses

The picture is of a mother
doting on the young child
she is hugging, the child smiling
with the look of promise in his eyes,
the one his mother wishes for him,

a nice child, bright faced
looking into the future with his child's
vision, his mother in rapture
with the promise of it all.

The mother is all around the world,
Iran, Ecuador, Syria, Ukraine, Mozambique,
Chile, et cetera. It doesn't matter where because
it is just the global, parental hand of love

no matter what the child may become, the love
of mother for child, universal even though at times
the power lords of the world do not judge it so,
and some of those children may grow up
into men somehow installed

in unimaginably grotesque lives
filled with the bullet-holes of poverty
and dead end lives—religious pawns
to the King of something malicious—
an unfortunate affiliation, a snare

with a seeming lock on everything
that casts them into the projectiles
that can carry them so far from the child
in the picture, the one that had once
so warmed his mother's heart.

Betrayal

The man accused of a heinous act
stands when the jurors enter,

his demeanor causes some in the courtroom
to think he is sociopathic-to-the-bone,
while others wonder about the act

that led to him standing, alone, there,
seemingly unrepentant to the degree

that it fires up anger in the hearts of some of those
beholders of the man's fate, and when he sits

down in response to his defender's gesture
in accordance with the established courtroom decorum,

he glares over his shoulder at the jurors seated
off to the side, his eyes an admix of shadow and a fury

never before witnessed by many jurors,
his grimace a tokened threat delivered

right to the chinks in the hearts of those subpoenaed there,
those now in whose hands the accused life is, those

unfamiliar with the man's existence, his back alley ways
and lead-poisoning, his single mother upbringing and gang
initiation, and acceptance to the newfound lifestyle there

in the war zones his childhood endured, the what-the-fuck
lack of hope that courses through his veins now, the nightmares
in the blackest of black.

Showtime

As I sat in the darkness and watched
the show of human form taking over
written form, I couldn't help but wonder
about art in such a transitory form. I
thought about the actors given to such
an art form that is so fleeting, evaporating
by the end of the work, and which can only live
on in the memory of those who were its witnesses,
there in the dark theater with its rows
of now emptying chairs, an exodus of just a flock
of minds now, while the actors backstage remove
their makeup and stage clothes that had assisted
them in the theatrical magic of the evening,
and then prepare to do their own dance
into the dark reality of their lives outside
the theater doors.

Good Day

you drew my attention quickly
like what I imagine the vision

of an angel would do, there
just outside the closed front window,

a silent entrance there on the lip
of concrete below the window with your look—

that of a curious alien
to my world—seeming to wait patiently

for something with your full-colored display
and black and yellow stripes crowning your head, noble

in a curious way, unafraid of my staring face
on the other side, your image warmed my heart

and wrenched me from my loneliness, so much so
that I had to resist the urge to open the window

and invite you in, my newfound friend, but the harsh
reality of our separateness stood in the way

while I remembered how many such beautiful birds I killed
with my bb gun as a young boy in the forest of my childhood,

in order to come as close as this.

Some Things

For every person or object, a shadow,
but only with the sun's permission.
For every tide, the moon lends force.

Through nightshades, stars gather dreams
and cast them down upon us, ones we
can fall into, or from which we can rise.

Shorelines give us magical stones
from the Earth's crucible, and, like children
we are enthralled by their shiny, colorful
solid forms.

All part of the world we walk in,
we learn instinctively to savor any light
beamed on black soil that can be,

with some luck someday, a field
of sunflowers lighting our way.

undelivered

words become morose   when unspoken
stillborn   and   much like rocks
on an abandoned plain
that exist only
in one geologic dimension
but aren't recognized in another
because they have never been seen,
they are without
receptive witnesses—words and rocks—
and bear the same
fate

Time is a curious messenger

of facts, slippery slants
of perception, now as I sit
contemplating the colorful, intricate
design of the room's Persian rug,
the black piano, elephant figurines,
the art from India adorning the walls,

all objects of a bona fide earthly nature,
of things as imagined by Lucretius, testaments
of the human spirit, of human endeavor in sculpture,
craft and weave, everything essential,
masterworks shaken loose from their creators,
now transported here before me, tokens
of everything ideal in the heart of things,
gifts of wisdom and integrity,

so that their songs resonate
around a soul.

To a Wonderful World

So everyone, in this simulated, walking-
tour course, it's super-important
that you relax and take a deep breath

before you gear-up with your goggles,
as you prepare to take the wheel (so-to-speak)
on your journey through the terrain you're

about to explore today. Now place your goggles
and adjust them to a secure but comfortable fit
to better insure a broad-range take on all the scenery

around you, to wit a more realistic
experience of all the richest of detail around you
as you take your virgin run on this high tech

equipment, one just short of something like Space X,
but with this you are tethered to Earth
and fully able to enjoy being here in the relative comfort

of this studio room. So, ready to-make your trip,
but remember to relax and breathe deeply,
please now as we begin to explore things

you've never seen before. Ah, yes, yes, here is a figure
on a street corner in all fairness looking tousled
and forlorn, a shadowy vision of a man lost

who asks for money from passersby who, with few exceptions,
pay him neither money nor heed, despite the audible pleas
on his part (Can you hear them through your double-sensory,

binaural headsets with their utterly superior pickup?)
Yeah, just relax and breathe deeply, and take it all in,
just as if you were watching a movie—just like it's make-believe!

Okay then, now we'll travel to an area of town where smallish
houses abound and—Watch this, guys!—we are

actually able to do a room-to-room search where each room seems
orderly and fairly well appointed. Then, at the end of the hallway,
we enter a bedroom with a desk, and we see a twenty-something

white male absorbed in counting bullets for several clips
for what appears to be a sleek, gray-black assault rifle leaning
against his desk. Yes, class, remember to relax and breathe deeply,

as we watch the man leave his house to either go hunting
or to a shooting range, and it is here that we should wish
the young man well in his pursuit of his own personal

fulfillment. We can even magically wave goodby and feel
good about his efforts to achieve satisfaction in his life.
As the man heads in to his day, we can now move on

to our next vision and feel warmed to come across a gaggle
of well appointed white men dressed in nothing but the finest
of suits, chatting away, shaking hands following their
    conversations,

and passing envelopes to one another. Notice that in the
    background
the majestic dome of our U.S. Congress rises (Oh what a beautiful
vision to behold in this wonderful country of ours, right?) Think
    God,

we're fortunate to live in a nation where well-dressed politicians
    can
take so much charge of our best dreams and our lives! Ah yes,
    again breathe
deeply and just relax, because everything's gonna be alright in

this alternate world reality just waiting for us out there in our most
beloved America!

Faith

the blurred lines between us
carry defined yet undefined aspirations—
fixedly premeditated, trustingly adorned
with the ultimate wishes that all is well,
that all can be in good faith, even bold
and broad takes on you and me in this
strange and fleeting dance of life, one
that is in sync, one that is loaded with
a music all its own that in good times
could give life wings.

On the Color Blue

blue is the soul of the artist
who if s/he were cast into other life
pursuits might become even
bluer—

think Billie Holiday who sang jazz
blues-style;
think Louis Armstrong's bluesy rendition
of *What a Wonderful World;*
think Van Gogh, Lorca, Plath and others who
turned a cold cheek to every pursuit
but art on the wings of angels in blue;
blue is the last conversation not knowing
it was the final one to be had with a departed soul

blue on the flip-side is the deep ocean
blue, afternoons of powder-blue sky,
the gleaming bright blue of a treasured
blown glass artwork

we so dream of some happy realm, but
sometimes must settle for a clouded, blue
haze as we navigate our time on Earth

Things Said

Can anesthetize the tongue,
Create musical metaphor,
Cajole,
Burn a should like a hot poker iron,
Kindle love in a lover's heart like
The music from a Gypsy's violin,
Stoke a war and, later,
Entreat peace,
Project blame, admit past sins,
Turn around a life teetering on
The edge of despair,
Raise a child from newborn—
Mentor a new spirit.

Ascent

The clarion call is out:
We must dust ourselves off
from the ashcans of past illusions.
We can and will construct
the seemingly unimaginable,

just as Leonardo da Vinci dreamed
of the bamboo and silk wings with which man
could fly someday,

just as the Dutch
dreamed of and constructed
a brilliant system of dykes and technical
innovations to control and manage
the North Sea that could have inundated their
civilization forever.

From the scary realm
people have/can and will rise
emboldened with the experience
of having fallen, even into the deepest
ashes.

Reconciliation

even if the road I have taken
even if I erred along the way
even if joy only embraced me
a part of the time,

my path in life I cannot regret
for my choices were made
on the wings of forces
of the unknown—by the mysterious
guardians of my soul, by a muse
here or there, perhaps by a callous
destiny whispering the route
in my ear.

all told, this road taken may be just,
suitably tailored for this maverick
in this place and time and space

even if I didn't have a majority share
in all the decisions along the way.

A Song for Earth from Outer Space

It might be thought that from 248 miles out
the Earth would just look like a fixed, blue
land-speckled globe, or maybe a giant blue-brown
taw poised and ready to reorder the the solar system.

On second glance, it really is stunning with its wink
to all the other planets around it. But then, when the micro view
pulls one's attention to all the souls scampering about in its
droughts, its famine, its pandemic-laced imbroglios and strife,
and the tribal habits of warfare among virtually all of its people,
there is a quiet pause.

The astronauts, privileged enough to glimpse
at our third planet from the Sun, can pause to marvel
at its beauty, and are fortunate during their temporary
high tech detachment from the lunatic conventions
and global realities abounding around the sphere far below them,
the one nestled fixedly, a pure marvel to behold.

About the Author

Stephen Anderson is a Milwaukee poet and writer whose work has appeared in *Southwest Review, Latin American Literature Today, Amsterdam Quarterly, Verse Wisconsin, Foundling Review, Twist in Time, Tipton Poetry Journal, New Purlieu Review, Free Verse, Poetica Review, Moss Piglet, Life and Legends, The Milwaukee Journal Sentinel, Lothlorien Poetry Journal, Verse Virtual, Blue Heron Speaks, Your Daily Poem, Blue Heron Review,* as well as in numerous other print and online journals. He was the recipient of the First Place Award in the Wisconsin Fellowship of Poets 2005 Triad Contest, and he received an Honorable Mention in the WFOP's 2016 Chapbook Contest. Many of his poems have been featured on the Milwaukee NPR affiliate WUWM Lake Effect Program. Anderson is the author of three chapbooks, as well as three full length collections with Kelsay Books, *In the Garden of Angels and Demons* (2017), *The Dream Angel Plays the Cello* (2019), and *High Wire* (2021). In the summer of 2013, six of his poems formed the text for a chamber music song cycle entitled *The Privileged Secrets of the Arch* performed by some musicians from the Milwaukee Symphony Orchestra and an opera singer. Anderson's work is being archived in the Stephen Anderson Collection in the Special Collections Section of the Raynor Memorial Libraries at Marquette University.

www.ingramcontent.com/pod-product-compliance
Lightning Source LLC
Chambersburg PA
CBHW072049160426
43197CB00014B/2688